ENGAGING WITH POLITICS

Other Books in the LIVING PROUD! Series

Being Transgender

Coming Out and Seeking Support

Confronting Stereotypes

Facing Homophobia

Finding Community

Keeping Physically Healthy

Living with Religion and Faith

Staying Mentally Healthy

Understanding Sexual Orientation and Gender Identity

LIVING PROUD! GROWING UP LGBTQ

ENGAGING WITH POLITICS

Robert Rodi and Laura Ross

**Foreword by Kevin Jennings
Founder, GLSEN (the Gay, Lesbian & Straight
Education Network)**

MASON CREST

Mason Crest
450 Parkway Drive, Suite D
Broomall, PA 19008
www.masoncrest.com

Copyright © 2017 by Mason Crest, an imprint of National Highlights, Inc. All rights reserved. No part of this publication may be reproduced or transmitted in any form or by any means, electronic or mechanical, including photocopying, recording, taping, or any information storage and retrieval system, without permission in writing from the publisher.

Printed in the United States of America

First printing
9 8 7 6 5 4 3 2 1

Series ISBN: 978-1-4222-3501-0
Hardcover ISBN: 978-1-4222-3504-1
ebook ISBN: 978-1-4222-8377-6

Cataloging-in-Publication Data is available on file at the Library of Congress.

Developed and Produced by Print Matters Productions, Inc. (www.printmattersinc.com)
Cover and Interior Design by Kris Tobiassen, Matchbook Digital

Picture credits: 10, World History Archive/Newscom; 17, Wikimedia Creative Commons; 18, Wikimedia Creative Commons; 26, Terry Schmitt/UPI/Newscom; 38, Jeff Malet Photography/ Newscom; 43, Wikimedia Creative Commons
Front cover: Jim Lo Scalzo/EPA/Newscom: Equality flag unfurled in front of the Supreme Court in June 2015 just before the landmark marriage equality decision was announced.

ENGAGING WITH POLITICS

CONTENTS

KEY ICONS TO LOOK FOR

Text-Dependent Questions: These questions send the reader back to the text for more careful attention to the evidence presented there.

Words to Understand: These words with their easy-to-understand definitions will increase the reader's understanding of the text while building vocabulary skills.

Series Glossary of Key Terms: This back-of-the-book glossary contains terminology used throughout this series. Words found here increase the reader's ability to read and comprehend higher-level books and articles in this field.

Research Projects: Readers are pointed toward areas of further inquiry connected to each chapter. Suggestions are provided for projects that encourage deeper research and analysis.

Sidebars: This boxed material within the main text allows readers to build knowledge, gain insights, explore possibilities, and broaden their perspectives by weaving together additional information to provide realistic and holistic perspectives.

FOREWORD

I loved libraries as a kid.

Every Saturday my mom and I would drive from the trailer where we lived on an unpaved road in the unincorporated town of Lewisville, North Carolina, and make the long drive to the "big city" of Winston-Salem to go to the downtown public library, where I would spend joyous hours perusing the books on the shelves. I'd end up lugging home as many books as my arms could carry and generally would devour them over the next seven days, all the while eagerly anticipating next week's trip. The library opened up all kinds of worlds to me—all kinds of worlds, except a gay one.

Oh, I found some "gay" books, even in the dark days of the 1970s. I'm not sure how I did, but I found my way to authors like Tennessee Williams, Yukio Mishima, and Gore Vidal. While these great artists created masterpieces of literature that affirmed that there were indeed other gay people in the universe, their portrayals of often-doomed gay men hardly made me feel hopeful about my future. It was better than nothing, but not much better. I felt so lonely and isolated I attempted to take my own life my junior year of high school.

In the 35 years since I graduated from high school in 1981, much has changed. Gay–straight alliances (an idea my students and I pioneered at Concord Academy in 1988) are now widespread in American schools. Out LGBT (lesbian, gay, bisexual, and transgender) celebrities and programs with LGBT themes are commonplace on the airwaves. Oregon has a proud bisexual governor, multiple members of Congress are out as lesbian, gay, or bisexual, and the White House was bathed in rainbow colors the day marriage equality became the law of the land in 2015. It gets better, indeed.

So why do we need the Living Proud! series?

- Because GLSEN (the Gay, Lesbian & Straight Education Network) reports that over two-thirds of LGBT students routinely hear anti-LGBT language at school

- Because GLSEN reports that over 60% of LGBT students do not feel safe at school
- Because the CDC (the Centers for Disease Control and Prevention, a U.S. government agency) reports that lesbian and gay students are four times more likely to attempt suicide than heterosexual students

In my current role as the executive director of the Arcus Foundation (the world's largest financial supporter of LGBT rights), I work in dozens of countries and see how far there still is to go. In over 70 countries same-sex relations are crimes under existing laws: in 8, they are a crime punishable by the death penalty. It's better, but it's not all better—especially in our libraries, where there remains a need for books that address LGBT issues that are appropriate for young people, books that will erase both the sense of isolation so many young LGBT people still feel as well as the ignorance so many non-LGBT young people have, ignorance that leads to the hate and violence that still plagues our community, both at home and abroad.

The Living Proud! series will change that and will save lives. By providing accurate, age-appropriate information to young people of all sexual orientations and gender identities, the Living Proud! series will help young people understand the complexities of the LGBT experience. Young LGBT people will see themselves in its pages, and that reflection will help them see a future full of hope and promise. I wish Living Proud! had been on the shelves of the Winston-Salem/Forsyth County Public Library back in the seventies. It would have changed my life. I'm confident that it will have as big an impact on its readers today as it would have had on me back then. And I commend it to readers of any age.

Kevin Jennings
Founder, GLSEN (the Gay, Lesbian & Straight Education Network)
Executive Director, Arcus Foundation

GLSEN®

GLSEN is the leading national education organization focused on ensuring safe and affirming schools for all students. GLSEN seeks to develop school climates where difference is valued for the positive contribution it makes to creating a more vibrant and diverse community. www.glsen.org

Bayard Rustin, one of Dr. Martin Luther King's principal lieutenants and chief organizer of the March on Washington, was an openly gay man.

1

THE HISTORY OF IDENTITY POLITICS

 WORDS TO UNDERSTAND

Bigotry: The stubborn and complete intolerance of a religion, appearance, belief, or ethnic background that differs from one's own.

Conservatives: Those who want to keep things the way they have always been; tending to be hostile to change and wanting to preserve tradition.

Homophobia: Fear and dislike of gay people.

Grassroots: At a local level; usually used in reference to political action that begins within a community rather than on a national or global scale.

As Adrienne Hudek explored the United States Holocaust Memorial Museum, she was moved by the many displays illustrating the horrors suffered by Jewish people. Then she saw a display about Nazi persecution of homosexuals from 1933 to 1945. As she stood and read the details of how thousands of gay people were murdered, she was shocked.

"That's something people don't talk about so much," she says. "I can't believe that ever happened. But it's important for us to remember that it did, so we can stop these things from happening again."

It may seem unlikely that such a thing *could* happen again. Today, popular culture is full of positive LGBT icons, such as musician Sir Elton John and television host Ellen DeGeneres. Rainbow-colored displays celebrate LGBT pride across the country during annual festivals. And with access to a diverse collection of viewpoints and information on the Internet, people are becoming increasingly familiar with—and comfortable with—LGBT issues and their relationship to national politics.

But these positive strides are a relatively recent development in the evolution of LGBT equality. For centuries, fear, hatred, and prejudice against LGBT people have run rampant; many have used their interpretation of the Bible's teachings as a weapon against LGBT people. Even today, despite growing acceptance and understanding, the fight for LGBT rights continues in the United States and around the world. In some places, including Saudi Arabia and Iran, homosexuality is still punishable by imprisonment or even death.

Understanding the history of LGBT issues can begin with something as simple as defining the term *homosexual*. While today it commonly refers to sexual attraction to people of one's own gender, the meaning has changed significantly over time.

CLOSE-UP: THE GAY HOLOCAUST

Today, the Holocaust is remembered as the Nazi slaughter of approximately six million European Jews during World War II. People often forget, though, that the Holocaust also included the Nazis' systematic murder of millions of people from other groups—including homosexuals.

Between 5,000 and 15,000 German homosexuals were sent to concentration camps. The Nazi government declared that homosexuals were contrary to "wholesome popular sentiment," and were consequently regarded as "defilers of German blood." The Gestapo (the Nazi police) raided gay bars, tracked individuals using the address books of those they arrested, and encouraged people to scrutinize the behavior of their neighbors and report suspected homosexual behaviors. Tens of thousands of gays were convicted between 1933 and 1944 and sent to camps for "rehabilitation," where they were identified first by yellow armbands and later by pink triangles worn on the left side of their jackets and right pant legs. Hundreds were castrated (their genitals mutilated) by court order; others were humiliated, tortured, used in hormone experiments conducted by Nazi doctors, and killed.

After the war, the full extent of gay suffering was slow to be revealed. Many victims kept their stories to themselves because homosexuality remained a criminal offense in postwar Germany.

Homosexuality as a Disorder

The word *homosexual* rarely appeared in print until 1926, when the *New York Times* became the first major American publication to use the term. At that time, homosexuality was considered a medical disorder or mental illness. Young people who acted upon their homosexual feelings—or even just admitted to having them—were often placed in institutions and subjected to horrific medical treatments in an attempt to "cure" the so-called illness.

But as time moved forward, experts began to speak out about these practices. In 1935, pioneering psychiatrist Sigmund Freud wrote in a letter that homosexuality "is nothing to be ashamed of, no vice, no degradation, it cannot be classified as an illness . . . it is a great injustice to persecute homosexuality as a crime."

This statement was reprinted in the *American Journal of Psychiatry* in 1951, but it would take another twenty-two years before the Board of Directors of the American Psychiatric Association removed "homosexuality" from its *Diagnostic and Statistical Manual of Mental Disorders* (DSM). And that wasn't the end of the story: It was replaced with another variation on the diagnosis, called "ego-dystonic homosexuality." Homosexuality wasn't removed entirely from the DSM until 1986.

Regardless of definitions and medical terms, **bigotry** has continued to touch the lives of LGBT people in the United States and around the globe. In their schools, churches, and even their homes, some young people still hear that being LGBT is wrong, a disease, and something of which to be ashamed. Numerous Christian organizations exist to "cure" individuals of homosexuality, though most have now been discredited—including Exodus International, a nonprofit formed in the 1970s that claimed to offer freedom from homosexuality through the power of Jesus Christ. It shut down in 2013. JONAH, a

Jewish organization that claims to use psychological techniques to free "strugglers" from homosexual desires, is still active.

The Stonewall Riots

The modern LGBT rights movement began in 1924 with the short-lived Society for Human Rights, the first recognized gay rights organization in the United States. But it wasn't until the 1950s that LGBT people began to get organized and build a movement with momentum. Mid 20th-century pioneers included Harry Hay, founder of the Mattachine Society, and Phyllis Lyon and Del Martin, who founded the Daughters of Bilitis. After years of public protests and increasing debate over equal rights, the movement finally caught fire in 1969, sparked by what would later be known as the Stonewall Riots.

The riots began after a police raid on June 28, 1969, at the Stonewall Inn, a gay bar in Greenwich Village in New York City. Known as one of the few gay-friendly areas of New York City, Greenwich Village was widely considered a safe haven for individuals looking to meet and socialize with other LGBT people, without fear of reprisal or attack. Or, at least, there was less fear.

At that time, police raids on gay bars were common. Many LGBT people were resigned to periodic harassment and the fear that they might be exposed and prosecuted. But with the growing force of the African-American Civil Rights Movement and anti-war demonstrations, people were feeling increasingly empowered to stand up for equal rights and fair treatment.

CLOSE-UP: THE FIRST LGBT RIGHTS ORGANIZATIONS

GLAAD, HRC, and other political alliances were the first LGBT advocacy groups to enjoy measurable successes. But they built on the groundwork of several courageous organizations that came before them and attempted to change a world vastly more hostile to gay people and gay issues.

The Society for Human Rights was founded in Chicago in 1924 by Henry Gerber—who was himself inspired by Magnus Hirschfeld's Scientific-Humanitarian Committee, a German group that Gerber encountered while serving abroad during World War I. The Daughters of Bilitis was a lesbian-rights group formed in 1955. The Mattachine Society was founded in Los Angeles in 1950 by pioneering activist Harry Hay; by 1961 it had grown large enough to divide into regional groups. The Mattachine Society was still active in the late 1960s, but its methods were seen as too conservative by the radical new activist organizations. We owe these pioneering groups a great debt for the bravery and foresight of their founders and members.

"Stonewall is the beginning of a true movement where we said, 'I will not let you harass, beat, and arrest me just because you don't like me.' Of the big things that happened in 1969, such as the moon landing, Stonewall is remembered," says Sabrina Sojourner, who became the first openly lesbian African-American to hold the title of U.S. Representative when she was elected as the "shadow" representative from the District of Columbia. "It could have been forgotten. Instead, it inspired generations."

Sabrina Sojourner represented three minority groups—blacks, women, and lesbians—when she was elected to the U.S. House of Representatives.

Early in the morning, police officers slammed through the doors of the Stonewall Inn, shouting for the two hundred patrons inside to line up to have their identification checked. Instead, the people in the bar refused. Frustrated at the injustice of being repeatedly harassed simply for being LGBT, they began to protest. Soon, dozens more people joined in from the street. As the crowd grew more and more restless, police quickly lost control of the situation. The *Daily News* featured the headline "3 Cops Hurt as Bar Raid Riles Crowd" and included this information (buried on page 30):

> *A predawn police raid on a reputed Greenwich Village homosexual hangout, the second raid within a week, touched off a two-hour melee yesterday as customers and villagers swarmed over the plainclothes cops. Before order was restored, the cops were the targets of thrown coins, cobblestones, and uprooted parking meters, windows were smashed, a police van was nearly overturned and the front of the raided bar, the Stonewall Inn, was fire-bombed.*

The Stonewall Inn, a symbol of pride for the gay community, was made an official landmark by New York City in 2015.

Rioting and protesting carried over into the next evening, as thousands of people turned up to support a seminal event in the LGBT rights movement.

"Before Stonewall, you took your life in your hands when you tried to be openly gay," recalls Martin Duberman, author of the book *Stonewall*. "Whenever we celebrate pride, a component of that pride should be that we are proud of our history and struggle and (that we) fought back against oppression and managed to have lives under that difficulty."

On the first anniversary of the riots, that feeling was embodied in the country's first Gay Pride march. The event, which was held in Greenwich Village, filled fifteen city blocks with peaceful marchers carrying signs and banners. Similar marches were held in Los Angeles and Chicago at the same time.

CLOSE-UP: THE CIVIL RIGHTS MOVEMENT'S GAY HERO

The African-American Civil Rights Movement was at a peak between 1955 and 1965. Martin Luther King, Jr., among others, led the fight to change American laws and attitudes.

The chief organizer of the historic 1963 March on Washington, and one of Dr. King's principal lieutenants, was an openly gay man, Bayard Rustin. Rustin's insistence on living openly as a gay man was very unusual at the time. Opponents of the Civil Rights Movement used his sexual orientation to attack him and the movement. He would not hide his sexual identity, however. So to protect the movement from these attacks, he generally worked behind the scenes providing crucial support and advice. After King's death, Rustin became an advocate of human rights and LGBT causes. He died in 1987, and was posthumously awarded the Presidential Medal of Freedom by Barack Obama in 2013.

The LGBT Rights Movement—and Its Backlash

The following year, numerous cities joined in the celebration that now continues annually around the globe. LGBT pride parades have become festivals highlighted by musical performances and speeches from activists and civil-rights leaders. Families and supporters of the LGBT community join in to celebrate diversity with banners, costumes, and colorful balloons. All of this followed from that groundbreaking day at the Stonewall Inn.

But as with all steps forward, these events also drew protests from religious and political **conservatives**, enraged at such a positive celebration of LGBT rights.

In the early 1970s several politicians came out after being elected to office, paving the way for an LGBT candidate to campaign openly and win election. That watershed event came in 1977, when openly gay politician Harvey Milk was elected to the San Francisco Board of Supervisors. (A year later, Milk was murdered by an anti-gay political adversary, and became one of the movement's first martyrs.)

By 1980, a political action committee called the Human Rights Campaign (HRC) was formed to raise money for congressional candidates who supported fairness for the LGBT community. The organization grew into one of the largest LGBT civil rights advocacy groups in the United States.

In response to the growing demand for equal rights, anti-gay activists, such as singer Anita Bryant, increasingly spoke out against homosexuality. As the leader of a group called Save Our Children, often considered the country's first national anti-gay group, Bryant frequently campaigned to strip away the limited rights and protections granted to the gay community. She soon became a human symbol of intolerance, bigotry, and **homophobia**. At that same time, author James Dobson founded Focus on the Family, which grew into America's wealthiest fundamentalist ministry and led the movement against marriage equality.

Other vocal opponents of LGBT rights included Reverend Jerry Falwell, founder of the Moral Majority, and Pat Buchanan, the communications director for President Ronald Reagan, who claimed that AIDS was "nature's revenge on gay men."

The Impact of the AIDS Crisis

Perhaps the most significant event to impact the LGBT rights movement was the AIDS epidemic that darkened the 1980s. First discovered in the late 1970s and thought to affect only gay men, it was originally called "gay cancer" or GRID (gay-related immune deficiency). This name immediately linked homosexuality with a deadly disease—a misunderstanding that caused a major setback in the battle for the equal rights of homosexuals. Religious extremists used the illness as evidence of God's displeasure with the "gay lifestyle," fanning the flames of fear and uncertainty that were sweeping the nation. As a result, more focus was placed on the epidemic as a gay issue than a medical issue, causing a severe delay in proper education about prevention and self-protection.

The medical community, though, recognized that the condition was not limited to homosexuals. In 1982, after more than 200 U.S. cases had been reported, the Centers for Disease Control officially recognized it as AIDS (short for acquired immune deficiency syndrome). Some researchers and doctors wanted to educate people about how it was transmitted and how it could best be avoided. They wanted to develop tests, treatments, and even a cure for the deadly disease—but it seemed that the world wasn't listening. President Ronald Reagan did not use the term *AIDS* in public until September 17, 1985, when he announced that funding would finally be provided for AIDS research. By that time, more than 5,500 deaths had already been identified in the United States.

Over thirty years after the beginning of the epidemic, the Kaiser Family Foundation estimates that more than 580,000 people have died in the United States and more than 1.7 million people have been infected with HIV (human immunodeficiency virus), the virus that causes AIDS. In the 1987 book *And the Band Played On: Politics, People and the AIDS Epidemic,* journalist Randy Shilts directly attributes the rapid spread of AIDS in America to the mistreatment of the gay community, both by legislative officials and the medical community, which delayed a proper and proactive response. The book received high critical acclaim and quickly became a bestseller.

"The numbers of AIDS cases measured the shame of the nation," Shilts writes. "The United States, the one nation with the knowledge, the resources, and the institutions to respond to the epidemic, had failed. And it failed because of ignorance and fear, prejudice and rejection. The story of the AIDS epidemic was that simple . . . it was a story of bigotry and what it could do to a nation."

Despite the scientific and medical evidence proving that AIDS was by no means limited to homosexuals, the initial association of

AIDS/HIV with the gay community all but halted the advancement of social equality.

The Gay Response to AIDS: Organize

But from this dark time in American history emerged some notable organizations that have had a significant impact on LGBT issues and politics. The Gay and Lesbian Alliance Against Defamation (GLAAD) was formed in 1985 to protest the *New York Post*'s coverage of the epidemic. Since then, the organization has played a large role in changing the way the LGBT community is portrayed in media and entertainment.

As these organizations sprang up, the LGBT community developed more of a voice in politics; local, state, and national groups began to respond to issues of homophobia, marriage equality, workplace discrimination, hate crimes, and the military's "Don't Ask, Don't Tell" policy, which stated that gay people had to be closeted while serving in the U.S. armed forces. Through grassroots movements and online information–sharing, growing numbers of LGBT community members and supporters continue to speak out to achieve equal rights.

Antigay Hate Crimes

These groups took center stage when the horrific torture and murder of Matthew Shepard captured headlines across the country and brought homophobia back into the spotlight. Shepard, a twenty-one-year-old student at the University of Wyoming, was offered a ride late one night in October 1998. After admitting he was gay, he was brutally beaten, then roped to a fence and left on a deserted road unconscious and near death. News of the attack swept the nation, prompting candlelight vigils and prayer sessions as Shepard struggled to survive in intensive care. He died on October 12, 1998, five days after the attack.

LGBT organizations were successful in getting Americans to view Shepard's murder as a hate crime—meaning that his attackers were motivated specifically by their hostility toward his sexual orientation.

Hate crimes have a long history in the United States. Our first hate-crime laws were passed in 1871, to combat the racially motivated crimes being committed against African Americans following the Civil War. But up until Matthew Shepard's case, the term was used to refer to crimes triggered by race, nationality, or religion. There was initial resistance to including sexual orientation as a legitimate category for hate-crime legislation. But thanks to diligent work by GLAAD, HRC, the Matthew Shepard Foundation, and other LGBT advocacy organizations, the Matthew Shepard and James Byrd, Jr. Hate Crimes Prevention Law was signed into law by President Obama in 2009.

In a tape recording he made to be played in the event of his assassination, Harvey Milk said, "I would like to see every gay doctor come out, every gay lawyer, every gay architect come out, stand up and let the world know. That would do more to end prejudice overnight than anybody would imagine. I urge them to do that, urge them to come out. Only that way will we start to achieve our rights."

TEXT-DEPENDENT QUESTIONS

- What factors turned an ordinary police raid of a gay bar into the history-making Stonewall Riots?

- How did the AIDS crisis affect the LGBT rights movement?

- How did Matthew Shepard's murder energize the LGBT rights movement?

 RESEARCH PROJECTS

- Compare the original Civil Rights movement with the LGBT Rights movement; make a list of similarities and differences in their goals, agendas, and strategies.

- Read more deeply about the trailblazing work done by the Society for Human Rights, the Mattachine Society, and the Daughters of Bilitis.

- Check out which states currently have hate-crime laws on their books, and who exactly is covered by such laws (i.e., all LGBT people or only certain groups?).

Jim Obergefell, the plaintiff in the Supreme Court decision that legalized same-sex marriage in all 50 states, rides as guest of honor in the Pride parade in San Francisco on June 28, 2015, shortly after the landmark decision was announced.

2
MARRIAGE EQUALITY

 WORDS TO UNDERSTAND

Nullified: No longer valid.
Controversy: A dispute, argument, or debate, especially one concerning a matter about which there is strong disagreement evident in public discourse or in the press.
Liberal: Open to change and new ideas.

Just like most grooms, Rob Kelly was nervous on his wedding day. Friends had come in from out of town, and he wanted everything to go right. As his sisters helped him get ready for the most important day of his life, he looked in the mirror over and over again, fixing his hair and making sure he looked perfect. He took a deep breath, thought of spending his future with his best friend, and made the happy and joyful walk down the aisle.

The ceremony had it all: vows, a minister, flowers, friends and family, matching rings, and, most importantly, a couple in love.

The only thing missing was the marriage license.

"We had a wedding with gifts and a reception, the whole thing," says Kelly, who held a marriage ceremony with his partner, Sean, in 2007. The wedding was not considered a legal union, however, because New York State didn't recognize marriage equality at the time. "I don't see how anyone can tell us we're not married, especially when it means that we don't get the same rights as straight couples."

But the United States government could, because of the Defense of Marriage Act (DOMA), which was signed into law by President Bill Clinton in 1996. DOMA held that no state had to honor same-sex marriages from other states, and that the federal government defined marriage as being a legal union between one man and one woman.

As the Human Rights Campaign pointed out, barring same-sex couples from federally recognized marriage denied them hundreds of basic protections and rights given to married heterosexual couples, including hospital visitation, Social Security benefits, immigration, health insurance, family leave, and pensions.

When Kenneth Johnson's partner James was rushed to the emergency room, Ken desperately sought information about his condition from the hospital staff—but they would only speak to immediate family. Even though Ken and James were registered as domestic partners in the state of California, he was told that they considered him "just a friend."

"At our covenant ceremony," Ken says, "I took James to be my life partner, 'for better or for worse, for richer or for poorer, in sickness and in health, to love and to cherish, until we are parted by death.' At the ceremony, I promised James, 'I'm not leaving, no matter what.'"

 CLOSE-UP: LGBT PARENTING

The last decade has seen a critical shortage of adoptive and foster parents, as well as a significant rise in the number of LGBT couples filing for adoption. Recognizing that LGBT couples can be exemplary parents, many agencies have cleared the way for LGBT adoptions. But, unlike marriage equality, adoption policy is still decided on a state-by-state basis. Most states allow for either joint adoptions (meaning that same-sex couples can adopt a child together so that both adults become the child's legal parents) or second-parent adoption (meaning that one person is declared the legal parent and the other can then adopt his or her partner's child and become a legal parent that way). Mississippi is the only state that restricts LGBT people from adopting. Activists are now advocating for a federal policy on LGBT adoption, along the lines of the marriage equality decision.

But he had to leave, to make the nearly three-hour drive home and back to get the documentation showing that James had given him power of attorney. Fortunately, he returned in time to spend precious last minutes with his husband, who died the following day. This is just one of thousands of examples of the pain and trouble people experienced when committed partners were not legally recognized.

Two Steps Forward...

The fight for marriage equality began decades earlier, in 1970, when University of Minnesota students Jack Baker and James Michael McConnell applied for a marriage license in Hennepin County, Minnesota. After the court clerk denied their request, they sued in District Court—and lost. They appealed to the State Supreme Court and lost again. They even took the case to the U.S. Supreme Court, but it was dismissed.

Their struggle is widely recognized as the first legal battle over the issue of marriage equality, but it was hardly the last. The years before and after DOMA saw a series of lawsuits, legal maneuvers, and court decisions aimed at determining each state's stance on marriage equality.

On Valentine's Day 2001, the organization Marriage Equality USA organized same-sex couples in Los Angeles, New York City, and San Francisco to apply for marriage licenses. All were declined. But San Francisco Mayor Gavin Newsom breathed new life into the movement in 2004, when he began issuing marriage certificates to same-sex couples attended by extensive media coverage. As a home to the nation's counter-culture since the 1950s, San Francisco had stood out as the center of the LGBT rights movement since the creation of the Castro, an urban LGBT neighborhood, and the election of openly gay activist Harvey Milk to the Board of Supervisors in the 1970s.

Although the California Supreme Court later **nullified** the San Francisco marriage licenses, the trend continued that same year when Massachusetts became the first U.S. state to legalize same-sex marriage.

By 2007, New Hampshire, Oregon, and Washington had advanced the cause of equality in their states by allowing civil unions or domestic partnerships for same-sex couples. The next year, the Supreme Courts of California and Connecticut recognized marriage equality, and in 2009, Iowa, Vermont, Maine, and New Hampshire legalized same-sex marriage, too. In 2010, marriage equality was recognized in the District of Columbia.

The decision by the California Supreme Court that same-sex marriage was legal under the state constitution gained national attention when thousands of couples were wed, including comedian Ellen DeGeneres and her partner, actress Portia de Rossi.

...One Step Back

But the ruling of the Supreme Court doesn't always reflect the will of the people. The decision stirred up **controversy** throughout California and across the country. Heated debates began, and groups claiming the need to protect families launched a campaign in support of Proposition 8. This measure, also known as the California Marriage Protection Act, stated that "only marriage between a man and a woman is valid or recognized in California." Less than five months—and thousands of weddings—after the Supreme Court's decision, California voters passed Proposition 8 on Election Day, November 2008. Marriage equality was no longer legal in the state of California.

"It (is) the first time in history that they would change the state constitution and take rights away. It's just amazing," said Ellen DeGeneres on her popular daytime talk show. "Here we're taking a giant step towards equality," she said, referring to the recent election of Barack Obama, our first African-American president, "and then this is happening, and I don't understand it."

But California was not alone in taking a step back on the issue of LGBT civil rights that year. Arizona and Florida voters also chose to outlaw marriage equality, making a total of thirty states that had passed such legislation.

Considering California's historically **liberal** leanings, with diverse cultural centers, such as San Francisco and Los Angeles, the show of intolerance there was especially surprising. In a statement responding to the Proposition 8 vote in California, actor George Clooney said, "At some point in our lifetime, gay marriage won't be an issue, and everyone who stood against the civil right will look as outdated as George Wallace standing on the school steps keeping James Hood from entering the University of Alabama because he was black."

A Civil Rights Issue

Many LGBT rights activists drew similar parallels to the black civil rights movements of the 1960s, when popular opinion was outweighed by the rule of Supreme Court. Ironically, though, the increased turnout of minority voters for the presidential election is thought to have sealed the fate of marriage equality in California, where exit polls showed that 70 percent of black voters supported the ban.

"We got married just a few days before election day, because we knew Prop 8 would pass," says Tom Brinkley, who married his partner in California in 2008. "I know there are people out there who don't understand gay marriage or who think it's a threat. But people felt the same way about interracial couples getting married forty years ago. If we'd listened to those people, just think what the world would be like today."

U.S. Congressman John Lewis, the youngest speaker at the 1963 March on Washington led by Dr. Martin Luther King, is among many civil rights leaders who saw the similarities in the struggle for LGBT rights. He frequently spoke out about the need for the same rights and equalities he fought for in the 1960s to be extended to the LGBT community.

"We cannot keep turning our backs on gay and lesbian Americans. I have fought too hard and too long against discrimination based on race and color not to stand up against discrimination based on sexual orientation," said Congressman Lewis in 2003. "I've heard the reasons for opposing civil marriage for same-sex couples. Cut through the distractions, and they stink of the same fear, hatred, and intolerance I have known in racism and bigotry."

CLOSE-UP: MARRIAGE EQUALITY'S REPERCUSSIONS

The 2015 Supreme Court decision creating marriage equality in all fifty states was an encouraging sign that the LGBT movement is winning its long battle for civil rights. But the ruling was not greeted with unanimous celebration. Social conservatives and religious extremists seemed energized by their defeat and vowed to fight harder to overturn it. One well-publicized example was Kim Davis, the Kentucky county clerk who defied the new law by refusing to issue marriage licenses to same-sex couples, citing her religious beliefs. She even did jail time rather than submit to a court order to perform her duties, thus becoming a kind of martyr for conservatives who compared her to Rosa Parks, the African-American woman who sixty years earlier triggered the Civil Rights movement by refusing to sit at the back of a bus. Many pundits countered that in fact, Davis had more in common with the racist bus driver who refused to drive until Parks got up and moved.

At Long Last, Victory

While the United States struggled with the idea, marriage equality became the law of the land in Belgium, Canada, the Netherlands, Spain, South Africa, Norway, Sweden, Argentina, Iceland, Portugal, Denmark, Brazil, the United Kingdom, France, New Zealand, Uruguay, Luxembourg, and Ireland. How could the Western world's most advanced democracy be so far behind? Especially since, in 2012, Barack Obama became the first sitting U.S. president to publicly declare his support.

That same year, Maine, Maryland, and Washington became the first states to legalize marriage equality through a popular vote. Also in 2012, Minnesota became the first state where voters rejected a constitutional amendment seeking to bar marriage equality. In 2013, the Supreme Court ruled that "federal law could not treat as unequal, marriages that individual States had created as equally valid," when it overturned a key provision of DOMA, thus forcing federal recognition of same-sex marriage and marriage-related benefits when related to a same-sex marriage performed by a state that sanctioned such marriages.

Over the subsequent two years, like a domino effect, a significant number of U.S. district and state courts issued rulings that marriage equality bans violated the Constitution. Support for marriage equality grew exponentially. Finally, on January 16, 2015, the U.S. Supreme Court agreed to hear a case on appeal—Obergefell vs.

Hodges—that directly addressed the constitutionality of marriage equality.

Six months later, a 5-4 majority of justices led by Anthony Kennedy, held that the Fourteenth Amendment requires states to permit same-sex marriages within their boundaries, and recognize the marriages of same-sex citizens from other states. In his majority opinion, Justice Kennedy wrote, "Decisions about marriage are among the most intimate that an individual can make. This is true for all persons, whatever their sexual orientation."

The court's four conservative members vigorously dissented, with Chief Justice Roberts taking the unusual step of reading his dissent from the bench. Justice Antonin Scalia's nine-page dissent went viral on the Internet—or at least its most blistering passages did, those in which he called the decision, among other things, a "threat to American democracy."

Enduring Past Death

But the long battle had been won, and as a result LGBT people today live in a world Jack Baker and James Michael McConnell could scarcely have dreamed of when they became the first same-sex couple to apply for a marriage license in 1970.

Andrew Sullivan, a gay political writer and author who has advocated for marriage equality since the 1990s, and who stopped writing his influential blog six months before the ruling, returned to it after

Obergefell vs. Hodges to pen an exuberant appreciation. His long post included the following passage:

> *I think of the gay kids in the future who, when they figure out they are different, will never know the deep psychic wound my generation— and every one before mine—lived through: the pain of knowing they could never be fully part of their own family, never be fully a citizen of their own country. I think, more acutely, of the decades and centuries of human shame and darkness and waste and terror that defined gay people's lives for so long. And I think of all those who supported this movement who never lived to see this day, who died in the ashes from which this phoenix of a movement emerged. This momentous achievement is their victory, too—for marriage, as Kennedy argued, endures past death.*

TEXT-DEPENDENT QUESTIONS

- Who was the first elected official to issue marriage certificates to LGBT couples?

- What was Proposition 8, and why is it unique in American history?

- Which state was the first to recognize marriage equality—and in what year?

 RESEARCH PROJECTS

- Check out the Fourteenth Amendment to the U.S. Constitution, which was cited by the Supreme Court in the decision that established marriage equality.

- Have a look at the Obergefell vs. Hodges decision, and pay attention to the arguments of the various judges.

- If you have LGBT friends who have married, or are engaged to be married, ask them about the difference they expect marriage will make (or has made) in their lives.

Protestors gathered near the White House in 2010 to demand a repeal of the ban on LGBT people serving in the military and the "Don't Ask, Don't Tell" (DADT) policy. Six service members handcuffed themselves to the White House fence.

3
LGBT PEOPLE IN THE MILITARY

 WORDS TO UNDERSTAND

Empirical evidence: Factual data gathered from direct observation.
Outed: Revealed or exposed as gay against one's will.
Ostracized: Excluded from the rest of a group.
Epithets: Words or terms used in a derogatory way to put a person down.
Stereotypes: Simplified, often negative, images applied to all members of a group (e.g., blondes are dumb).

Historic Congressional Cemetery in Washington, D.C., is the final resting place of nearly a hundred senators and representatives, as well as American patriots, such as John Philip Sousa, who composed "Stars and Stripes Forever" and "Semper Fidelis" and Robert Mills, who designed the Washington Monument. Among the notable memorials, there is a black stone marker that bears no name. Instead it reads, "When I was in the military they gave me a medal for killing two men and a discharge for loving one."

This is the grave of Leonard P. Matlovich, who served as a technical sergeant in the United States Air Force during the Vietnam War. He was awarded the Purple Heart and the Bronze Star. He taught Air Force Race Relations classes.

And he was gay.

Giving a Face to Gay Servicemen

Matlovich made headlines when he challenged the ban on homosexuals serving in the military. On Memorial Day in 1975, his personal battle became public knowledge with an article in the *New York Times* and a television interview with Walter Cronkite. On September 8, 1975, Matlovich appeared on the cover of *Time* magazine, accompanied by the declaration, "I am a homosexual."

The Air Force offered him the chance to remain in the military, provided he would sign a statement pledging never to practice homosexuality again. Matlovich refused. He sued for reinstatement but eventually settled when he believed it was clear that the conservative U.S. Supreme Court would deny his appeal. Instead, Matlovich dedicated his life to the gay rights movement.

"I found myself, little nobody me, standing up in front of tens of thousands of gay people," he told *Time*. "And just two years ago I thought I was the only gay in the world. It was a mixture of joy and sadness. It was just great pride to be an American, to know I'm oppressed but able to stand up there and say so."

The groundbreaking case brought the issue of gay men and women serving in the military into the spotlight. But some historians believe the issue took root centuries earlier, when homosexuals were dismissed from the U.S. military as far back as the Revolutionary War. Since then, gay soldiers have been court-martialed and discharged, either honorably or dishonorably. Often the dismissal bars them from receiving benefits, continuing the discrimination into civilian life.

Serving in Silence

At the time of Matlovich's groundbreaking court case, the policy of the U.S. military was to ask new recruits about their sexual orientation before they were permitted to serve. If service members were gay, or even suspected of being gay, they could be prosecuted and imprisoned.

"I recall looking hard at the word 'homosexual' on the entry form I filled out to enlist in the U.S. Air Force, then at the 'Yes' or 'No' boxes that followed the word. It seemed as though time stood still as I considered how to answer that question," recalls Garland Auton, who joined the Air Force in 1987.

As time went on, I continued to be dedicated, hard working, and professional, but I also started to be more afraid of being discovered as a gay man in the military. As my enlistment neared its end, I had to make a decision on whether to stay in the military and continue being afraid of who I was or to receive an honorable discharge and move on. I made my decision after re-reading a section of the Declaration of Independence: 'that all men are created equal, that they are endowed by their Creator with certain unalienable Rights, that among these are Life, Liberty and the pursuit of Happiness.' In order to pursue my happiness, I could no longer serve in the military. I could not continue to live a double life.

Many LGBT activists were hopeful in 1992, when then–presidential candidate Bill Clinton stated publicly that he opposed the military's exclusion of gay, lesbian, and bisexual soldiers. Many hoped that the silence would finally come to an end, and all Americans could serve their country openly. After Clinton's election, national debate on the issue raged across the country. LGBT rights advocates felt sexual orientation had no bearing on a person's ability to serve in the military. Hearings were held before the Senate Armed Services Committee, and the result was a compromise reached in 1993 that has come to be known as "Don't Ask, Don't Tell, Don't Pursue, Don't Harass."

"Don't Ask, Don't Tell"

The decision was far from a victory for LGBT rights. Although it prohibited recruiters and military authorities from asking about an individual's sexual orientation, it also stated that gays and lesbians could be discharged for making statements about their sexuality, either in public or in private, attempting to marry someone of the same sex, or if they were caught engaging in a homosexual act.

"The policy is an absurdity and borderlines on being an obscenity," said Clifford Alexander, Former Secretary of the Army.

The policy essentially asked people to lie to themselves, and pretend to be something that they are not. There is no **empirical evidence** indicating that it affects military cohesion. However, there is a lot of evidence to say that the biases of the past have been layered onto the United States Army.

To commemorate the 14th anniversary of the "Don't Ask, Don't Tell" policy, the Human Rights Campaign displayed 12,000 flags on the National Mall to recognize the men and women discharged from the military since the policy was enacted.

More than 13,000 individuals were discharged under the "Don't Ask, Don't Tell" policy, according to the Servicemembers' Legal Defense Network (SLDN), which estimates that this cost taxpayers more than a quarter of a billion dollars. Approximately one thousand of these individuals had been in highly necessary positions, including engineers and interpreters of Middle Eastern languages. Many of them later joined SLDN to fight the legal battle against this policy, including former U.S. Army Sergeant Darren Manzella. He served in the Combat Lifesaver program, training nonmedical soldiers in emergency first-aid procedures. While under fire in Iraq, he cared for injured soldiers and earned a Combat Medical Badge. Manzella was also threatened with being **outed** as gay and investigated under "Don't Ask, Don't Tell." He wrote:

> *I don't think most people can understand how hard it is to have to hide their true self; to have to pretend to be someone that they are not; to be scared that you'll be **ostracized** for being different; to be told that you're wrong if you live a certain life . . . that concerns no one else but yourself. . . . I am proud of myself and of the accomplishments I have achieved in my life. I know that being gay would not have made a difference in receiving my college degree . . . my time spent as a psychiatric counselor . . . [and] certainly didn't make a difference when I treated injuries and saved lives in the streets of Baghdad.*

SLDN studies also found that young adults between the ages of eighteen and twenty-five had become the group most significantly affected by this policy. In the Air Force in 2002, 83 percent of "Don't Ask, Don't Tell" discharges were in this age group.

Once such case involved Pfc. Barry Winchell, who died shortly before his twenty-second birthday after being attacked with a baseball bat in barracks at Fort Campbell, Kentucky. Witnesses reported that Winchell had been the victim of severe harassment and inquiries related to his sexuality. The incident occurred in 1999, six years after "Don't Ask, Don't Tell" was enacted. Such incidents were not uncommon.

"When I got out of the field and was released for the weekend, I walked to my truck and found a sign with 'FAG' written on it sitting on my windshield," says former Staff Sergeant Leonard Peacock, who served from 1995–2001.

*It concerned me, but I threw it away because I didn't want to attract attention. But the harassment didn't stop there. I got to my truck one day to see black stickers spelling out, "FAG," "RAINBOW WARRIOR," "GAY" and other **epithets** on my windshield. This experience in my new unit began to sour me on the military—there were so many people basing their judgments of me on **stereotypes.***

I would have enjoyed continuing my service, if we were all just treated equally. As it was, I put in more than six years. Being mistreated by so many other soldiers and being discharged from the military just because of one's sexual orientation is discrimination— plain and simple. I do not understand how our society allows it to happen, if we are all so advanced and civilized. What makes gay, lesbian, and bisexual soldiers different? We are not different; we all fight as soldiers. We all put our lives on the line, fighting for the same cause.

 CLOSE-UP: HARASSMENT OF LGBT SERVICE MEMBERS

In the post-"Don't Ask, Don't Tell" era, things aren't entirely rosy for gays in the military. In the first four years since the act's repeal, there were 4,600 reported cases of harassment of gay, lesbian, and bisexual service people; and while transgender men and women are at present still barred by federal law from serving, it seems likely that their inclusion in the ranks will only exacerbate the problem. A shocking 47 percent of surveyed LGBT veterans reported at least one experience of assault. The unfortunate result of these kinds of abuses—which include offensive speech, derogatory names, jokes, or remarks, as well as physical violence and property damage—is a chilling effect on the kind of openness the repeal of DADT was meant to encourage. For the moment, at least, being out while serving in the military is still a decision each service member has to weigh against potential risks.

Another major flaw in the policy was that there was no one—not even doctors or religious leaders—that gays and lesbians could talk to openly. Even psychotherapists and chaplains, who are supposed to keep people's secrets, were known to report service members dealing with issues of homosexuality, according to the Human Rights Campaign.

Repeal...and Respect

Such statistics and factors led many to question the effectiveness of the policy. A bill was introduced in the House in 2005 to repeal "Don't Ask,

Don't Tell," but it didn't make it out of committee. Three years later, more than a hundred retired generals and admirals spoke out in favor of ending the discriminatory policy. And in 2010, President Barack Obama included the issue in his State of the Union address.

We find unity in our incredible diversity, drawing on the promise en-shrined in our Constitution: the notion that we are all created equal, that no matter who you are or what you look like, if you abide by the law you should be protected by it. We must continually renew this promise. . . . This year, I will work with Congress and our military to finally repeal the law that denies gay Americans the right to serve the country they love because of who they are.

He was as good as his word. The act was repealed in December 2010. The legislation specified that the policy would remain in place until the President, Secretary of Defense, and Chairman of the Joint Chiefs of Staff had certified that its repeal wouldn't adversely effect military readiness; this certification was sent to Congress on July 22, 2011, which scheduled the end of the policy for September 20, 2011.

One year later, a study published by the Palm Center think tank found no evidence that openly gay servicemen and servicewomen had had any negative effect on the military. And on the repeal's first anniversary, the President reflected on the achievement.

A year ago today, we upheld the fundamental American values of fair-ness and equality by finally and formally repealing "Don't Ask, Don't Tell." Gay and lesbian Americans now no longer need to hide who they love in order to serve the country they love. It is a testament to the professionalism of our men and women in uniform that this change was implemented in an orderly manner, preserving unit cohesion, recruitment, retention and military effectiveness. As Commander in Chief, I've seen that our national security has been strengthened because we are no longer denied the skills and talents of those patriotic Americans who happen to be gay or lesbian. The ability of service members to be open and honest about their families and the people they love honors the integrity of the individuals who serve, strengthens the institutions they serve, and is one of the many reasons why our military remains the finest in the world.

 ## TEXT-DEPENDENT QUESTIONS

- For how long have gays, lesbians, and bisexuals been subject to dismissal from the American armed services?
- What exactly was meant by the phrase, "Don't Ask, Don't Tell"?
- In what ways was "Don't Ask, Don't Tell" a flawed policy?

 ## RESEARCH PROJECTS

- Visit LeonardMatlovich.com, the memorial page to the first American soldier to come out.
- Check out the policies toward LGBTQ servicemen and servicewomen in other countries around the globe.
- Search the Internet for some of the reactions—both pro and con—to the repeal of "Don't Ask, Don't Tell."

4

WORKPLACE ISSUES AND DISCRIMINATION

 WORDS TO UNDERSTAND

Stigma: A mark of disgrace or shame.

Ballot initiative: An opportunity for citizens to vote for or against something. A number of U.S. states allow for this procedure, whereby citizens are able to draw up a petition for a proposed change in the law; if they can get enough signatures, it will be put before voters.

Bias: A tendency or preference toward a particular perspective or ideology, when the tendency interferes with the ability to be impartial, unprejudiced, or objective.

As Chelsie Collins prepared for her prom, she had more on her mind than just finding a date. In fact, she had already found the perfect date. And that's when things got more complicated for the Alabama teen.

When Chelsie and her date, Lauren Farrington, announced their plans to attend the prom at Scottsboro High School, the news was not well received. Dr. Judith Berry, the school superintendent, and the Scottsboro City Board of Education told them they were not permitted to attend together. Rather than backing down, the Collins and Farrington families looked to the courts for assistance.

"The only reason they were not allowed to attend is that their sexual orientation was brought up," says Parker Edmiston, the attorney for the families.

Just hours before the event, the decision was made. "John Graham, circuit court judge here in Jackson County ordered that the Scottsboro Board of Education (and) its administrators could not deny these girls attending their prom," Edmiston recalls.

The decision was a blow to discrimination against LGBT teens. But the news was not all good. The same year in Wisconsin, an out gay teen nominated for prom queen was barred from runing for the title by his high school. Similar controversies continue to occur across the United States.

Standing Up to Discrimination

The history of discrimination in education and employment includes a number of individuals who bravely stood up against injustice. In 1957, when Dr. Franklin E. Kameny was fired by the U.S. Civil Service Commission from his post as an astronomer in the Army Map Service in Washington, D.C., because he was gay, he protested and argued his case in front of the U.S. Supreme Court. The episode has become known as one of the first major gay civil rights cases.

Employment discrimination had been around long before the historic Stonewall riots, when thousands of people protested increasing intolerance of the LGBT community in 1969. "Before Stonewall, for most lesbians and gay men, being open on the job was to invite an almost immediate dismissal and the **stigma** that came with it," says Bob Witeck, co-author of *Business Inside and Out*. "Workplaces were merely extended 'closets,' where gay men and lesbians concealed themselves completely, and made very sure to cover their tracks, and bring opposite-sex dates to company occasions and parties."

The Fight for Workplace Protection

Throughout the 1970s, individual businesses began making strides to ban workplace discrimination of gays and lesbians. The first legislation aimed at protecting gay rights was introduced into the House of Representatives in 1975, and, though it did not pass, it brought increasing attention to the issue.

In 1978, California State Senator John Biggs attempted a **ballot initiative** to ban gay teachers. "One third of San Francisco teachers are homosexual," Biggs announced at the time. "I assume most of them are seducing young boys in toilets."

The initiative failed, but **bias** and discrimination against homosexuals in the workplace continued. In 1982, Wisconsin became the first state to ban workplace discrimination of LGBT people in all employment. In the ensuing decades, nearly two dozen states followed suit, but a federal law that includes protection against discrimination on the basis of sexual orientation and gender identity is still on the horizon. In

1994, the Employment Non-Discrimination Act (ENDA) was proposed in the U.S. Congress. Modeled after the Civil Rights Act of 1964 and the Americans with Disabilities Act, ENDA calls for extending federal protection to include discrimination based on sexual orientation and gender identity. The law would apply to government employees, but would not affect small businesses with fewer than fifteen employees, religious organizations, or the military.

Although ENDA has been introduced in every Congress since 1994 except the 109th, it has yet to pass. As of 2015, discrimination based on sexual orientation or gender identity continues to be legal in twenty-eight states.

 CLOSE-UP: ENDA AND HOBBY LOBBY

In 2014, ENDA lost the support of some high-profile gay rights groups in the wake of the Supreme Court's controversial *Burwell v. Hobby Lobby* decision, which allows corporations to exempt themselves from laws that violate their religious beliefs. For Hobby Lobby (a chain of retail craft stores), this meant an exemption from including certain forms of birth control in their health care plan. The National Gay and Lesbian Task Force, Lambda Legal, and other LGBT advocacy groups feared that the broad religious exemptions in the bill would allow companies to fire or refuse to hire LGBT workers. The Task Force's executive director, Rea Carey, said, "If a private company can take its own religious beliefs and say you can't have access to certain health care, it's a hop, skip and a jump to an interpretation that a private company could have religious beliefs that LGBT people are not equal or somehow go against their beliefs and therefore fire them. We disagree with that trend. The implications of Hobby Lobby are becoming clear." Democrats have vowed to seek ways to address the Hobby Lobby decision through legislation.

Shattering the Workplace Closet

Jacqueline Thomas experienced such discrimination when she was working a temporary job at a law firm. Though she never told colleagues she was gay, they made the assumption. Among other jibes and insults, she was told that AIDS existed because of people like her. And there was nothing she could do but leave the job.

"I always have to balance the financial consequences of coming out with the psychological consequences of not coming out," she says. "Although American workplace tolerance is increasing toward gays and lesbians, we still meet with some outright hostility. But harassment on the basis of sexual orientation has no place in our society."

Despite the shortcomings of employment law, popular opinion and other legal decisions continue to make strides toward ending discrimination against LGBT people, whether in workplaces or at high school dances. In 2009, federal law was expanded to include gender identity and sexual orientation in hate crimes legislation. This means that crimes committed against someone because of race, religion, gender, ethnicity, nationality, sexual orientation, gender identity, and disability can be federally prosecuted.

"Hiding one's sexual orientation takes work. But not coming out can take a terrible toll on a person's self-esteem and personal happiness," Thomas says.

Winning the Battle Slowly But Steadily

LGBT rights organizations have taken a grassroots approach to protesting discriminatory organizations. Every year, the Human Rights Campaign releases a "Buying for Equality" list that encourages LGBT rights supporters to buy from businesses that have publicly stated employment policies that protect LGBT employees. The organization also publishes a Corporate Equality Index, rating hundreds of the nation's biggest employers on their benefits to LGBT employees.

"Now that we have an unprecedented opportunity to effect dramatic change for our community, it is more important than ever that we keep our allies in this fight close at hand," says Joe Salmonese, president of the Human Rights Campaign Foundation. "We can help seize this opportunity with the economic choices we make. Each time we spend money, we support one or more companies. We need to support our community with these choices. . . . [Our guide] shows which corporations support our community—through nondiscrimination policies, equal family benefits, comprehensive healthcare, and employee support—and which do not."

Many state and government agencies also continue to move forward to provide the workplace protections that Dr. Franklin Kameny fought so hard to achieve. And on June 29, 2009, more than fifty years after his dismissal, he was finally vindicated. In a ceremony hosted by the Office of Personnel Management (OPM), the renamed department that had fired him five decades earlier, OPM Director John Berry formally apologized to Kameny on behalf of the U.S. government. The statement was met with a resounding, "Apology accepted!" from the aged Dr. Kameny, who also received the Theodore Roosevelt Award, the department's most prestigious honor.

"With the fervent passion of a true patriot, you did not resign yourself to your fate or quietly endure this wrong. With courage and strength, you fought back," Berry wrote in the official letter presented to Dr. Kameny. "Please accept our apology for the consequences of the previous policy of the United States government, and please accept the gratitude and appreciation of the United States Office of Personnel Management for the work you have done to fight discrimination."

 TEXT-DEPENDENT QUESTIONS

- On what successfully passed acts is ENDA based?
- How does HRC use LGBT people's purchasing power to bring about equality?

 RESEARCH PROJECTS

- Look up your own state's policy regarding LGBT employment discrimination.
- Find an online history of ENDA and follow the full history of the attempts to pass it in Congress.

⊡ SERIES GLOSSARY

Activists: People committed to social change through political and personal action.

Advocacy: The process of supporting the rights of a group of people and speaking out on their behalf.

Alienation: A feeling of separation and distance from other people and from society.

Allies: People who support others in a cause.

Ambiguous: Something unclear or confusing.

Anonymous: Being unknown; having no one know who you are.

Assumption: A conclusion drawn without the benefit of real evidence.

Backlash: An adverse reaction by a large number of people, especially to a social or political development.

Bias: A tendency or preference toward a particular perspective or ideology that interferes with the ability to be impartial, unprejudiced, or objective.

Bigotry: Stubborn and complete intolerance of a religion, appearance, belief, or ethnic background that differs from one's own.

Binary: A system made up of two, and only two, parts.

Bohemian: Used to describe movements, people, or places characterized by nontraditional values and ways of life often coupled with an interest in the arts and political movements.

Caricature: An exaggerated representation of a person.

Celibate: Choosing not to have sex.

Chromosome: A microscopic thread of genes within a cell that carries all the information determining what a person is like, including his or her sex.

Cisgender: Someone who self-identifies with the gender he or she was assigned at birth.

Civil rights: The rights of a citizen to personal and political freedom under the law.

Clichés: Expressions that have become so overused—stereotypes, for example—that they tend to be used without thought.

Closeted: Choosing to conceal one's true sexual orientation or gender identity.

Compensating: Making up for something by trying harder or going further in the opposite direction.

Conservative: Cautious; resistant to change and new ideas.

Controversy: A disagreement, often involving a touchy subject about which differing opinions create tension and strong reactions.

Customs: Ideas and ways of doing things that are commonly understood and shared within a society.

Demonize: Portray something or someone as evil.

Denominations: Large groups of religious congregations united under a common faith and name, and organized under a single legal administration.

Derogatory: Critical or cruel, as in a term used to make a person feel devalued or humiliated.

Deviation: Something abnormal; something that has moved away from the standard.

Dichotomy: Division into two opposite and contradictory groups.

Discrimination: When someone is treated differently because of his or her race, sexual orientation, gender identity, religion, or some other factor.

Disproportionate: A situation where one particular group is overrepresented within a larger group.

Diverse: In the case of a community, one that is made up of people from many different backgrounds.

Effeminate: A word used to refer to men who have so-called feminine qualities.

Emasculated: Having had one's masculinity or manhood taken away.

Empathy: Feeling for another person; putting yourself mentally and emotionally in another person's place.

Empirical evidence: Factual data gathered from direct observation.

Empowering: Providing strength and energy; making someone feel powerful.

Endocrinologist: A medical doctor who specializes in the treatment of hormonal issues.

Epithets: Words or terms used in a derogatory way to put a person down.

The Establishment: The people who hold influence and power in society.

Extremist: Someone who is in favor of using extreme or radical measures, especially in politics and religion.

Flamboyant: Colorful and a bit outrageous.

Fundamentalist: Someone who believes in a particular religion's fundamental principles and follows them rigidly. When the word is used in connection with Christianity, it refers to a member of a form of Protestant Christianity that believes in the strict and literal interpretation of the Bible.

Gay liberation: The movement for the civil and legal rights of gay people that originated in the 1950s and emerged as a potent force for social and political change in the late 1960s and '70s.

Gender: A constructed sexual identity, whether masculine, feminine, or entirely different.

Gender identity: A person's self-image as female, male, or something entirely different, no matter what gender a person was assigned at birth.

Gender roles: Those activities and traits that are considered appropriate to males and females within a given culture.

Gene: A microscopic sequence of DNA located within a chromosome that determines a particular biological characteristic, such as eye color.

Genitalia: The scientific term for the male and female sex organs.

Genocide: The large-scale murder and destruction of a particular group of people.

Grassroots: At a local level; usually used in reference to political action that begins within a community rather than on a national or global scale.

Harassed/harassment: Being teased, bullied, or physically threatened.

Hate crime: An illegal act in which the victim is targeted because of his or her race, religion, sexual orientation, or gender identity.

Homoerotic: Having to do with homosexual, or same-sex, love and desire.

Homophobia: The fear and hatred of homosexuality. A homophobic person is sometimes referred to as a "homophobe."

Horizontal hostility: Negative feeling among people within the same minority group.

Hormones: Chemicals produced by the body that regulate biological functions, including male and female gender traits, such as beard growth and breast development.

Identity: The way a person, or a group of people, defines and understands who they are.

Inborn: Traits, whether visible or not, that are a part of who we are at birth.

Inclusive: Open to all ideas and points of view.

Inhibitions: Feelings of guilt and shame that keep us from doing things we might otherwise want to do.

Internalized: Taken in; for example, when a person believes the negative opinions other people have of him, he has *internalized* their point of view and made it his own.

Interpretation: A particular way of understanding something.

Intervention: An organized effort to help people by changing their attitudes or behavior.

Karma: The force, recognized by both Hindus and Buddhists, that emanates from one's actions in this life; the concept that the good and bad things one does determine where he or she will end up in the next life.

Legitimized: Being taken seriously and having the support of large numbers of people.

LGBT: An initialism that stands for lesbian, gay, bisexual, and transgender. Sometimes a "Q" is added (**LGBTQ**) to include "questioning." "Q" may also stand for "queer."

Liberal: Open to new ideas; progressive; accepting and supportive of the ideas or identity of others.

Liberation: The act of being set free from oppression and persecution.

Mainstream: Accepted, understood, and supported by the majority of people.

Malpractice: When a doctor or other professional gives bad advice or treatment, either out of ignorance or deliberately.

Marginalize: Push someone to the sidelines, away from the rest of the world.

Mentor: Someone who teaches and offers support to another, often younger, person.

Monogamous: Having only one sexual or romantic partner.

Oppress: Keep another person or group of people in an inferior position.

Ostracized: Excluded from the rest of a group.

Out: For an LGBT person, the state of being open with other people about his or her sexual orientation or gender identity.

Outed: Revealed or exposed as LGBT against one's will.

Persona: A character or personality chosen by a person to change the way others perceive them.

Pioneers: People who are the first to try new things and experiment with new ways of life.

Politicized: Aware of one's rights and willing to demand them through political action.

Prejudice: An opinion (usually unfavorable) of a person or a group of people not based on actual knowledge.

Proactive: Taking action taken in advance of an anticipated situation or difficulty.

Progressive: Supporting human freedom and progress.

Psychologists and psychiatrists: Professionals who study the human mind and human behavior. Psychiatrists are medical doctors who can prescribe pills, whereas clinical psychologists provide talk therapy.

Quackery: When an untrained person gives medical advice or treatment, pretending to be a doctor or other medical expert.

The Right: In politics and religion, the side that is generally against social change and new ideas; often used interchangeably with *conservative*.

Segregation: Historically, a system of laws and customs that limited African Americans' access to many businesses, public spaces, schools, and neighborhoods that were "white only."

Sexual orientation: A person's physical and emotional attraction to the opposite sex (heterosexuality), the same sex (homosexuality), both sexes (bisexuality), or neither (asexuality).

Sociologists: People who study the way groups of humans behave.

Spectrum: A wide range of variations.

Stereotype: A caricature; a way to judge someone, probably unfairly, based on opinions you may have about a particular group they belong to.

Stigma: A mark of shame.

Subculture: A smaller group of people with similar interests and lifestyles within a larger group.

Taboo: Something that is forbidden.

Theories: Ideas or explanations based on research, experimentation, and evidence.

Tolerance: Acceptance of, and respect for, other people's differences.

Transgender: People who identify with a gender different from the one they were assigned at birth.

Transphobia: Fear or hatred of transgender people.

Variance: A range of differences within a category such as gender.

Victimized: Subjected to unfair and negative treatment, including violence, bullying, harassment, or prejudice.

FURTHER RESOURCES

The American Gay Rights Movement
A short history.
civilliberty.about.com/od/gendersexuality/tp/History-Gay-Rights-Movement.htm

The American Gay Rights Movement: A Timeline
Major milestones from 1924 to the present.
www.infoplease.com/ipa/A0761909.html

Hate Crime Laws
A map showing the status of all fifty states.
www.lgbtmap.org/equality-maps/hate_crime_laws

Fighting Hate Crimes
A guide for taking action.
www.pbs.org/pov/beyondhatred/take_action.php

History of the Freedom to Marry In the United States
A timeline chronicling the arc of the marriage equality movement.
www.freedomtomarry.org/pages/history-and-timeline-of-marriage

Overview of Lesbian and Gay Parenting, Adoption, and Foster Care
A fact sheet from the American Civil Liberties Union.
www.aclu.org/overview-lesbian-and-gay-parenting-adoption-and-foster-care

Equality Maps
Summaries of laws that affect LGBT Americans on a state-by-state and issue-by-issue basis.
www.familyequality.org/get_informed/equality_maps/

Non-Discrimination Laws
A state-by-state map.
www.aclu.org/map/non-discrimination-laws-state-state-information-map

INDEX